Luke

Alfred's Premier Piano Course

Gayle Kowalchyk • E. L. Lancaster

Correlated Standard Repertoire

Alfred's Premier Piano Course: Masterworks 6 includes standard repertoire from the four stylistic periods to reinforce concepts introduced in *Lesson 6*. All pieces are in their original form and have not been adapted. Dynamics, phrasing, fingering, and pedal are editorial in some selections. The editors also have added titles to untitled pieces.

The pieces in this book correlate page by page with the materials in *Lesson 6*. They should be assigned according to the instructions in the upper right corner of selected pages of this book. They also may be assigned as review material at any time after the student has passed the designated lesson book page. In these pieces, terms or symbols that have not been used in *Lesson 6* are defined in footnotes or parentheses.

A compact disc recording is included with this book. It can serve as a *performance* model or as a *practice* companion. See information about the CD on page 40.

Performance skills and musical understanding are enhanced through *Premier Performer* suggestions. Students will enjoy performing these pieces for family and friends in a formal recital or on special occasions. See the List of Compositions on page 40.

Cover Design by Ted Engelbart
Interior Design by Tom Gerou
Music Engraving by Linda Lusk

ISBN-10: 0-7390-9342-8
ISBN-13: 978-0-7390-9342-9

Use with Alfred's Premier Piano Course,
Lesson Book 6, pages 4–5

Minuet in G Major

(from the *Notebook for Anna Magdalena Bach*)

CD 1/2

Johann Sebastian Bach
(1685–1750)

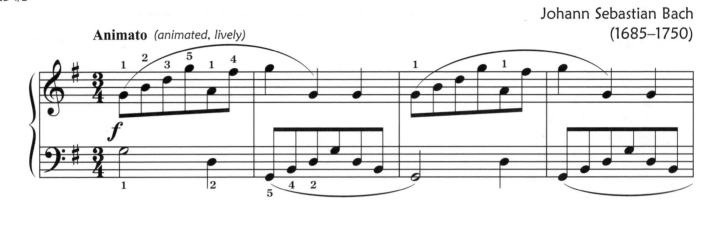

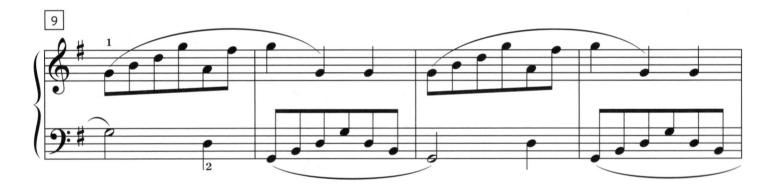

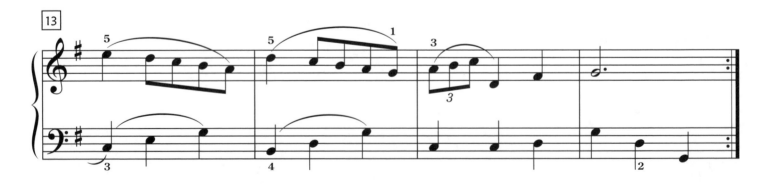

Premier Performer *Listen carefully for even eighth notes.*

Lesson Book: pages 6–7

Russian Polka*

CD 3/4

Mikhail Ivanovich Glinka
(1804–1857)

* A polka is a fast Bohemian dance in $\frac{2}{4}$ time that originated around 1830.

Premier Performer

Capture the spirit of the dance with crisp staccatos and strong accents.

The Cuckoo

CD 5/6

François Couperin
(1668–1733)

* ✼ The sixteenth rest is equal to the length of a sixteenth note.

** The dotted sixteenth note is almost always followed by a thirty-second note. In $\frac{3}{8}$ time, the dotted sixteenth note gets 3/4 of a beat and the thirty-second note gets 1/4 of a beat.

Dance in E-flat Major

CD 7/8

Christian Gottlob Neefe
(1748–1798)

Allegretto scherzando *(moderately quick, playful)*

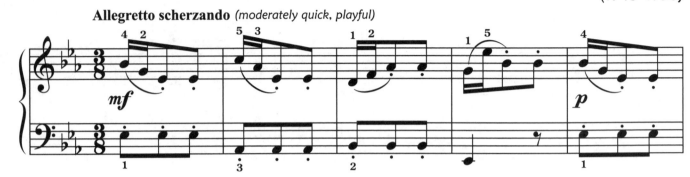

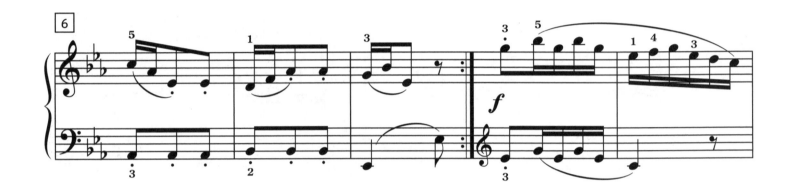

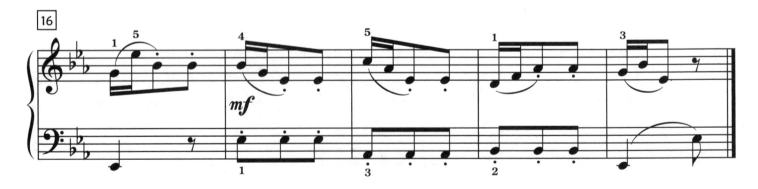

Premier Performer

Choose a tempo that allows you to feel one beat per measure.

Gypsy Dance
(Trio)

CD 9/10

Franz Joseph Haydn (1732–1809)
Hob. IX:28, No. 1

Premier Performer

Use strong fingers so that sixteenth notes are clear and even.

Stormy Seas

CD 11/12

Cornelius Gurlitt (1820–1901)
Op. 141, No. 14

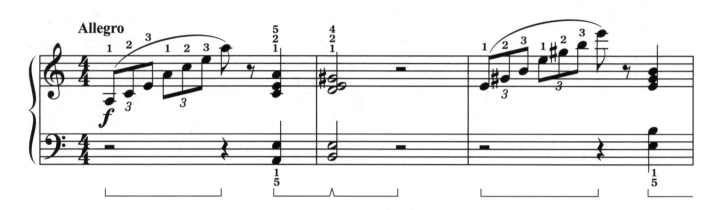

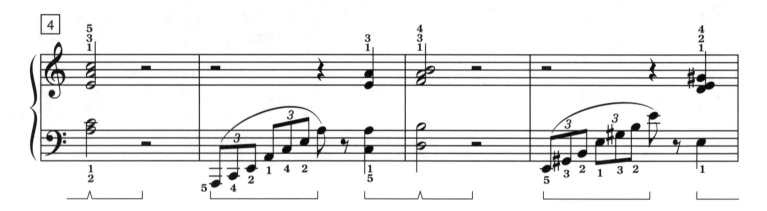

Premier Performer *Listen for smooth crossings in the arpeggios.*

Lesson Book: page 18

Melody

CD 13/14

Robert Schumann (1810–1856)
Op. 68, No. 1

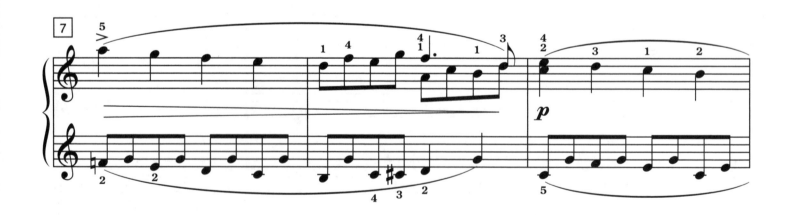

 Premier Performer

*Bring out the RH melody throughout.
The LH should sound like a duet part
and be a little softer than the RH.*

Lesson Book: pages 19–21

Chromatic Polka

CD 15/16

Louis Köhler (1820–1886)
Op. 300, No. 160

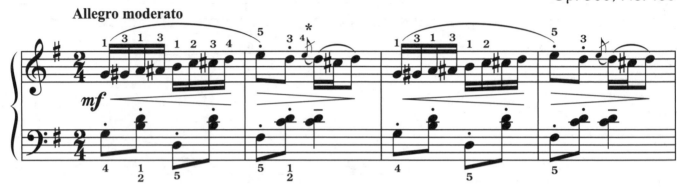

* Play the grace note quickly before the beat.

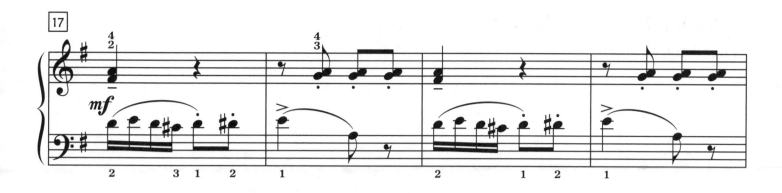

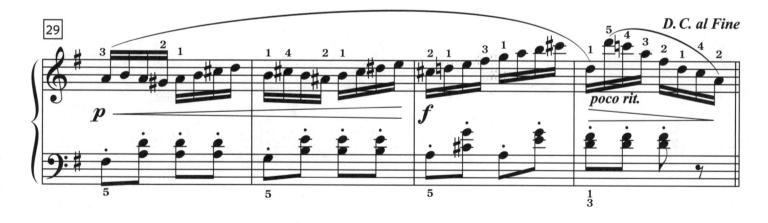

Premier Performer

Keep the sixteenth notes even and clear. Contract the hand so that fingertips 1, 2, and 3 remain close to one another in chromatic scale passages.

Lesson Book: page 22

Sonatina in F Major
(First Movement)

CD 17/18

Ludwig van Beethoven (1770–1827)
(Anh. 5, No. 2

* Play the grace note quickly before the beat.

(Second Movement)

CD 19/20

RONDO*

* A rondo is a multisection piece in which a theme is repeated several times.

** ♬ A group of four thirty-second notes equals an eighth note.

Lesson Book: pages 26–27

Waltz in E-flat Major

CD 21/22

Muzio Clementi
(1752–1832)

Premier Performer

*Play the LH softer than the RH
and staccato throughout.*

Lesson Book: page 28

Night Piece

CD 23/24

Hugo Reinhold (1854–1935)
Op. 39, No. 20

Premier Performer *Use the articulations and sudden dynamic changes to tell the story of a dark and mysterious night.*

Lesson Book: page 29

The Clown

CD 25/26

Vladimir Rebikov
(1866–1920)

Premier Performer *Create a playful mood with the slurs and crisp staccato notes.*

Lesson Book: page 34

Écossaise* in C Major

CD 27/28

Johann Nepomuk Hummel (1778–1837)
Op. 52, No. 5

* An écossaise is an English country dance in $\frac{2}{4}$ meter popular in the late 18th and early 19th centuries.

** Play the grace note quickly before the beat.

Premier Performer   *Play the LH with energy, but softer than the RH.*

Lesson Book: pages 36–37

German Dance in G Major

CD 29/30

Franz Joseph Haydn
(1732–1809)

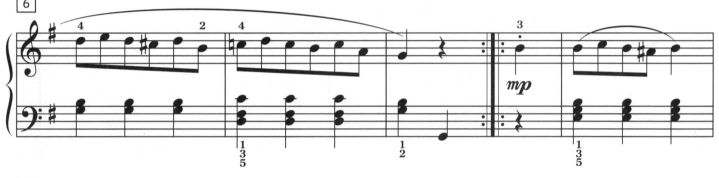

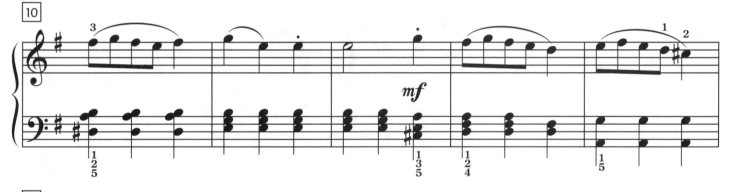

Lesson Book: pages 38–39

Allegro in F Major

CD 31/32

Franz Joseph Haydn (1732–1809)

Hob. III: 73/4

* *f–p* Play *forte* the first time through; play *piano* on the repeat.

Italian Song

CD 33/34

Lesson Book: pages 44–47

Peter Ilyich Tchaikovsky (1840–1893)
Op. 39, No. 15

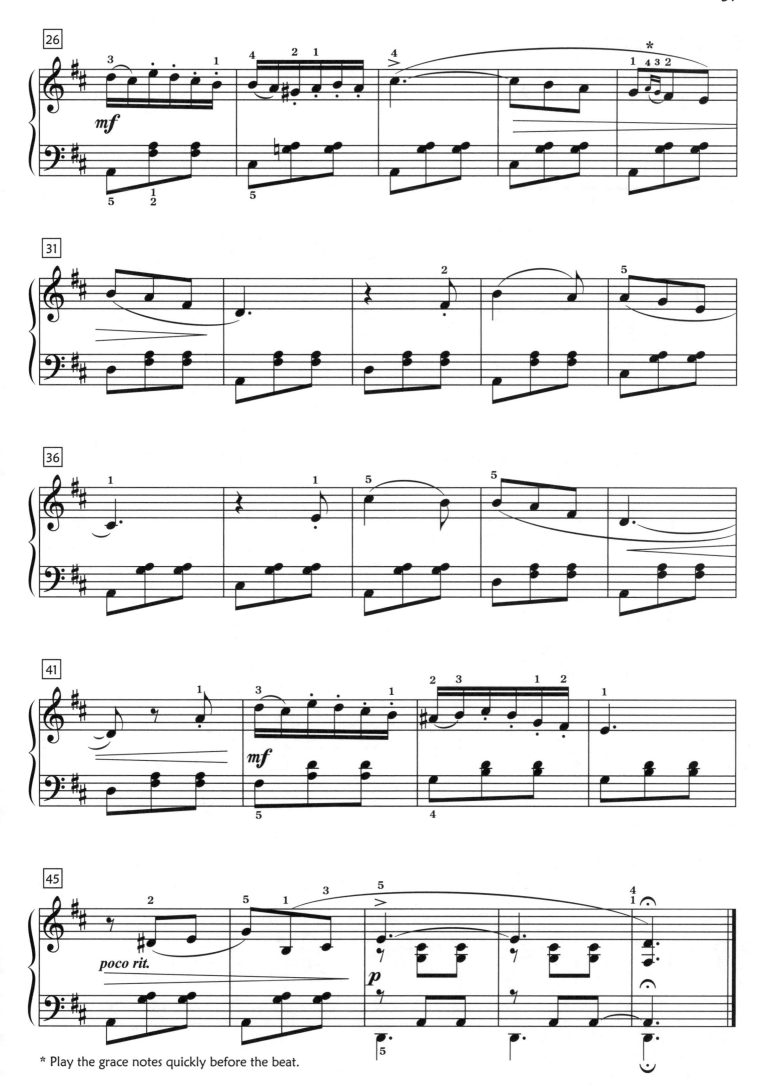

* Play the grace notes quickly before the beat.

Lesson Book: pages 48–49

Valsette

CD 35/36

Jean Sibelius (1865–1957)
Op. 40, No. 1

*Play the grace note quickly before the beat.

Premier Performer — *Imagine that the RH melody is being sung by a vocalist.*

Lesson Book: pages 50–53

Sonatina in A Minor

CD 37/38

Georg Anton Benda
(1722–1795)

Premier Performer

In measures 17–22, 33–34, and 37–38, bring out the LH melody.

Lesson Book: pages 54–55

Prelude in C Major

(from *The Well-Tempered Clavier, Book I*)

CD 39/40

Johann Sebastian Bach (1685–1750)
BWV 846

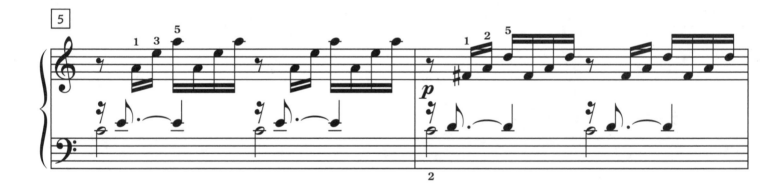

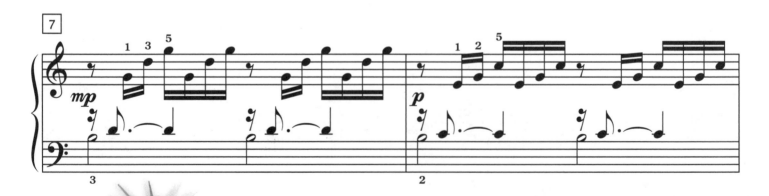

Premier Performer

Each two-beat pattern should sound as one continuous line, with the LH flowing seamlessly to the RH.

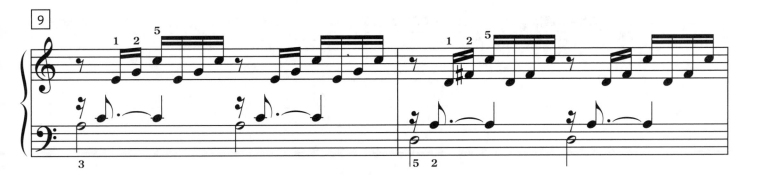

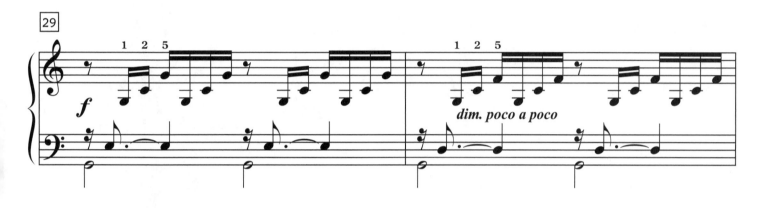

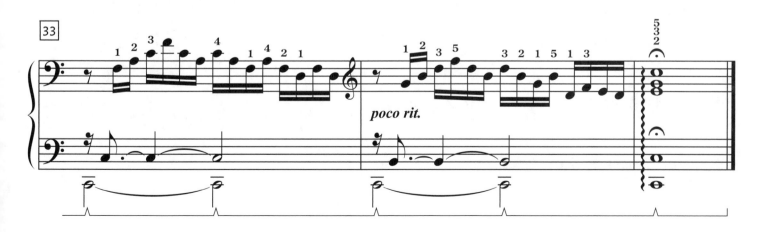

List of Compositions

Note: *Each selection on the CD is performed twice. The first track number is a performance tempo. The second track number is a slower practice tempo.*

The publisher hereby grants the purchaser of this book permission to download the enclosed CD to an MP3 or digital player (such as an Apple iPod®) for personal practice and performance.

Illustration by Jimmy Holder

CD Performances by Scott Price